AF615410

how to have fun cooking breakfast

By Editors of Creative

Illustrated by Melva Mickelson

DEDICATED TO
TOM, MIKE, KRISTY and TIMMY

Library of Congress Number: 73-18257
ISBN: 0-87191-291-0

Published by Creative Education, Mankato, Minnesota 56001.

Library of Congress Cataloging in Publication Data
Creative Educational Society, Mankato, MN
How to have fun making breakfast.
(Creative craft books)
SUMMARY: Includes simple breakfast recipes and suggestions for serving and setting the table.
1. Cookery — Juvenile literature. (1. Cookery) I. Title.
TX652.5.C68 1973 641.5'2 73-18257
ISBN 0-87191-291-0

ABOUT COOKING

Cooking food began with primitive man. Meat was probably the first food that he cooked after he learned to make a fire. Paintings have been found in caves of France and Spain and other ancient countries showing people of the Stone Age cooking their food.

When fireplaces were added to the home, cooking was brought indoors. The cooking utensils were made of iron.

Now with all of the modern stoves and appliances food can be prepared in many fast and easy ways. Imagine what a pioneer woman would say if she could see food cooked in a microwave oven!

ABOUT BREAKFAST

You have probably heard your mother or some other grown up tell you that you must eat breakfast. Why? Breakfast is the meal that begins our day.

Breakfast is not the same all over the world. In fact, your breakfast is probably even different than some of your friends. In Europe many people have an early breakfast of sweet rolls with coffee or hot chocolate. Later they have another breakfast. In England breakfast is usually cooked porridge (a cooked cereal), toast, marmalade (jelly or jam), tea and a meat such as kidneys, or cooked sausage. In the United States breakfast is usually fruit or fruit juice, cereal, coffee and toast. Some people include bacon and eggs or pancakes and sausages.

Our breakfast cereal has not always been in boxes and ready to eat. Only since the 1900's has cereal been available in this instant form. Before this time most cereal was cooked and served warm. You have probably had a cooked cereal such as oatmeal, or cream of wheat yourself.

TOASTED
CORN
FLAKES

LET'S BEGIN

Cooking is fun. But, many things must be taken care of before you are ready to begin cooking.

Always begin by deciding what you want to make. If you are going to cook breakfast, plan the entire meal. Then, check to be sure you have everything that you need to prepare your breakfast.

Read each recipe. Gather all ingredients and utensils. Then you will be ready to begin. When you finish be sure to put all ingredients away, wash the utensils and clean the kitchen.

The recipes that follow are recipes for cooking some of the most popular breakfast foods. Try cooking these several times. You may want to begin by doing only the bacon one day. The next day try scrambling eggs or fixing pancakes.

After you have practiced all of these you will be ready to have fun making the entire breakfast.

EASY COOKING

Let's start by making toast. This is fun and very easy.

You will need:

- bread
- toaster
- butter
- butter knife
- paper towels

Choose the kind of bread you like best. Put it in the toaster. Set the toaster so that it will toast the bread the way you like it . . . light or dark. Push the toaster down and wait for the toast to pop up. When it is done lay the toast on a piece of paper towel. Butter your toast, cut it and it is ready to eat, or add jelly and peanut butter.

CINNAMON
SUGAR
Peanut
Butter

Fixing cold cereal is very easy.

You will need:

- cereal
- a cereal bowl
- a cereal spoon
- milk
- sugar (if the cereal is unsweetened)

Choose your favorite cold cereal. Place it in a bowl. If it needs sugar, add sugar and then put milk on it. Fruit can also be placed on top of your cereal.

Cooking bacon is easy but must be done carefully. Grease can spatter and burn you.

You will need:

- a fry pan
- bacon strips
- fork
- paper towels

Begin by placing bacon strips in a frying pan. You do not need any shortening in the frying pan. Place the frying pan on the stove on low heat. Cook the bacon slowly and turn it often with a fork. It is done when it is crisp and brown. Don't let it get too brown. Remove the bacon from the pan using a fork. Shut the burner off. Place the bacon on folded paper towels or napkins that will soak up the grease.

CHAMPION
OF BREAKFAST
JOHN
6

There are many ways to fix eggs. Here are two ways that are not too difficult for you to do.

Fried Eggs

You will need:

- eggs
- small dish
- fry pan
- 2 tablespoons fat or shortening
- spoon
- pancake turner
- salt and pepper

If you have just fried bacon, remove all of the fat left in the frying pan from the bacon, except 2 tablespoons. Or, put in 2 tablespoons of shortening. Place the frying pan on the stove. Turn the burner on medium. Break your eggs, one at a time, into a small dish. Empty the eggs, one at a time, into the frying pan. Turn the stove down onto a low setting. Cook the eggs slowly for about 5 minutes. As the eggs are

cooking, take a spoon and spoon some of the hot fat over the top of the eggs. This will help the top of the egg to cook. Salt and pepper the top of each egg lightly. The egg is done when the white of the egg is completely white and hard. The yellow part of the egg will be soft but not runny. Turn the burner off. Use a pancake turner to remove the egg from the pan and put it onto the plate.

Scrambled Eggs

This recipe will serve 3 people. Use 2 eggs for each person.

You will need:

- 6 eggs
- small mixing bowl
- ¾ teaspoon salt
- ⅛ teaspoon pepper
- mixing spoon
- frying pan
- wooden spoon

Put into your mixing bowl the eggs, salt and pepper. Beat these ingredients until the eggs are completely mixed.

Put a frying pan on the stove. Put in 3 tablespoons of butter or margarine. Turn the burner on medium.

When the frying pan is hot, pour the egg mixture in. Now turn the burner down on low. With a wooden spoon, scrape the mixture from the bottom and sides of the frying pan as it thickens. Continue this until the eggs are light and fluffy throughout. Turn the burner off. Remove eggs from the pan.

Pancakes

Pancakes are not hard to make. You can buy a pancake mix or use this recipe. Have fun watching the pancakes cook.

You will need:

- medium sized mixing bowl
- 1 cup sifted flour
- 1 teaspoon baking powder
- 1 tablespoon sugar
- ¾ teaspoon salt
- 1 egg
- 1 cup milk
- 2 tablespoons melted shortening
- ½ teaspoon baking soda
- griddle or frying pan
- pancake turner
- mixing spoon
- 1 cup measuring cup

Put in a medium sized mixing bowl –

1 cup sifted flour

1 teaspoon baking powder

1 tablespoon sugar

¾ teaspoon salt

½ teaspoon baking soda

Now, add

1 egg – well beaten

1 cup milk

2 tablespoons melted shortening

Prepare a griddle or a frying pan. If using a griddle ask mother if it needs shortening. If using a frying pan, add just a little shortening. When the griddle is hot, use a 1 cup measuring cup to put the batter onto the griddle. Leave about 1 inch between each pancake. When the pancakes are puffed up and full of bubbles, turn them over using a pancake turner. Bake on this side until it is browned. Remove with a pancake turner and stack on a plate. Serve when they are warm.

SERVING BREAKFAST

After you have practiced making the different recipes you will be ready to try making a complete breakfast.

Plan on doing this on a Saturday or Sunday when you will have time to prepare everything.

Begin with your menu. Check to see that you have everything you need. Begin with this menu:

Orange Juice
Toast and Jelly
Cereal
Bacon
Scrambled Eggs
Milk

When you are ready to begin, start by setting the table. Use placemats or a tablecloth and add a centerpiece of some kind to brighten the table.

In the middle of the table you can set the salt and pepper, butter dish, jelly or jam, sugar, fruit for cereal and a pitcher of milk.

Then the table should be set according to the diagram below. All hot foods will be put right on the individual plates. The juice glass can be left out if you are serving fresh fruit. Do not put out any of the dishes, glasses or flatware you will not be using. Be sure that the sharp edge of the knife is facing the plate.

Now, get out all ingredients and utensils. If you are having frozen fruit juice rather than fresh, you can even prepare this the night before. Follow the directions on the can. Leave it in the refrigerator so that it will be cold for morning.

Begin by frying your bacon. As the bacon is frying mix up your scrambled eggs. At this time have everyone begin breakfast with cereal and fruit juice. When the bacon is done you can cook the scrambled eggs. When the eggs are done, turn the burner off but leave the pan on the stove. Then put your bread into the toaster. While the bread is toasting put the bacon and eggs on each person's plate. Tell them to begin eating as soon as they have been served. By this time your toast will be ready. Butter and place it on a plate to pass. Pour milk into the glasses. Put your frying pan in water to soak while you are eating. Have fun eating and enjoying the compliments.

get organized
1.
2.
3.
4.
5.
6.

HAPPY DAY
MOTHER

Now you are in for a special treat. There is nothing more fun than having someone enjoy the food you cook. And, what a pleasant way to surprise mother when she's tired or not feeling well. You could even serve her breakfast in bed. The more you cook the more fun you will have and the easier it will be for you to prepare other foods.

how to have fun

BAKING COOKIES AND CAKES

BUILDING SAILBOATS

KNITTING

WITH MACRAME

MAKING BIRDHOUSES AND FEEDERS

MAKING BREAKFAST

MAKING CHRISTMAS DECORATIONS

MAKING KITES

MAKING MOBILES

MAKING PAPER AIRPLANES

MAKING PUPPETS

WITH NEEDLEPOINT

SEWING

WEAVING

WITH AN INDOOR GARDEN

creative craft books